Rivers and Lakes

Nile River

Cari Meister

ABDO Publishing Company

visit us at
www.abdopub.com

Published by ABDO Publishing Company, 4940 Viking Drive, Edina, Minnesota 55435.
Copyright © 2002 by Abdo Consulting Group, Inc. International copyrights reserved in
all countries. No part of this book may be reproduced in any form without written
permission from the publisher.

Printed in the United States.

Photo credits: Corbis

Contributing editors: Bob Italia, Tamara L. Britton, Kate A. Furlong, Kristin Van Cleaf
Book design and graphics: Neil Klinepier

Library of Congress Cataloging-in-Publication Data

Meister, Cari.
    Nile River / Cari Meister.
        p. cm. -- (Rivers and lakes)
    Includes bibliographical references.
    Summary: Surveys the origin, tributaries, history, plant and
animal life, and the Aswan Dam of the Nile River.
    ISBN 1-57765-098-0
    1. Nile River Valley--Juvenile literature. [1. Nile River
Valley.] I. Title. II. Series.
DT115.M45   2000
962--dc21   98-029324

Contents

The Nile River 4

The White Nile 6

The Blue Nile 8

The Atbara 10

Plants & Animals 12

The Nile Long Ago 14

Exploring the Nile 16

Taming the Nile 18

The Nile Today 20

Glossary 22

How Do You Say That? 23

Web Sites 23

Index 24

The Nile River

*T*he Nile River is the longest river in the world. It is 4,187 miles (6,737 km) long. The Nile has been important to plants, animals, and people for thousands of years. Millions of people have used its water for farming, drinking, and transporting both people and goods.

The Nile's **source** is the Kagera River in Burundi, Africa. The Nile travels through nine African nations on its long journey north. It flows through Lakes Victoria, Kyoga, Albert, and Nasser. The Nile's **mouth** is in Egypt, at the Mediterranean Sea.

The mighty Nile is fed by many **tributaries**. The most important are the Blue Nile, the White Nile, and the Atbara River.

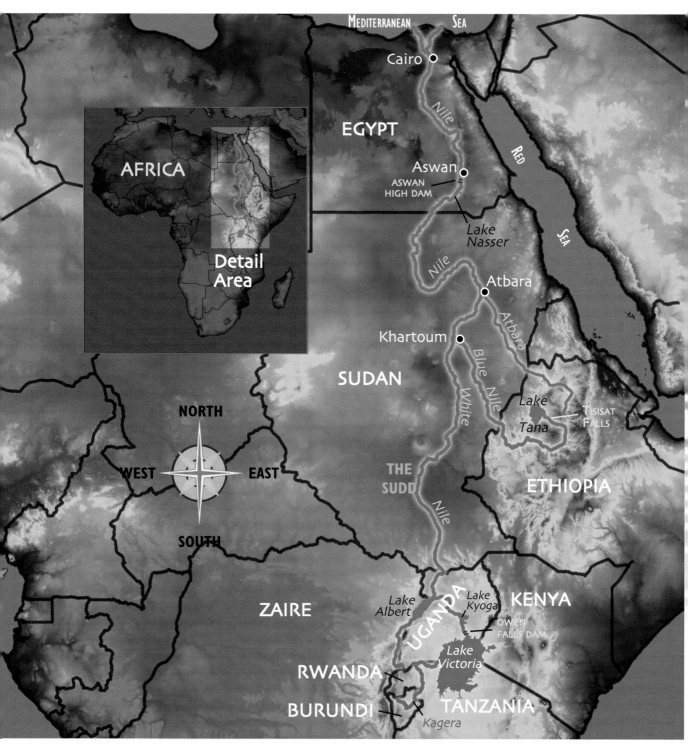

MEDITERRANEAN SEA

Cairo ○

EGYPT

Nile

RED

Aswan ○
ASWAN
HIGH DAM

SEA

Lake
Nasser

Nile

Atbara ○

Atbara

Khartoum ○

SUDAN

Blue Nile

White

Lake
Tana

TISISAT
FALLS

THE
SUDD

ETHIOPIA

Nile

AFRICA

Detail
Area

NORTH

WEST · EAST

SOUTH

ZAIRE

Lake
Albert

Lake
Kyoga

KENYA

UGANDA

OWEN
FALLS DAM

RWANDA

Lake
Victoria

BURUNDI

TANZANIA

Kagera

The White Nile

*T*he White Nile is the Nile River's longest **tributary**. It supplies about one-fourth of the Nile's water.

The White Nile starts in Uganda, at Lake Victoria. After the White Nile leaves the lake, it is called the Victoria Nile. It flows through Uganda and most of Sudan.

In Sudan, the river enters Lake Albert. After the river leaves Lake Albert, it is called the Albert Nile. Then the river enters a low, flat area called the Sudd. The Sudd is the world's largest swamp. Here, the White Nile loses much water to **evaporation**.

After the White Nile leaves the Sudd, it reaches the city of Khartoum, Sudan. There, the White Nile joins with the Nile's next great tributary, the Blue Nile.

Homes on the shore of Lake Victoria

The Blue Nile

*T*he Blue Nile supplies more than half of the Nile River's water. The Blue Nile begins in the Ethiopian highlands. Its **source** is near Lake Tana. From Lake Tana, the Blue Nile flows north.

Soon the river reaches Tisisat Falls. From there, it enters a deep **gorge**. In some places, the gorge is almost 5,000 feet (1,524 m) deep. The water moves through the gorge quickly.

After leaving the gorge, the Blue Nile widens and moves more slowly. When the river reaches Khartoum, Sudan, it joins the White Nile to form a single river, called the Nile.

From Khartoum, the Nile River continues northward. At Atbara, Sudan, it joins with the Nile's last great **tributary**, the Atbara River.

Tisisat Falls

The Atbara

*T*he Atbara River is the Nile's last major **tributary**. The Atbara's **source** is in the Ethiopian highlands north of Lake Tana. From there, it flows 500 miles (804 km) to Atbara, Sudan.

During flood season, heavy rains in the Ethiopian highlands cause the Atbara to rise. The floodwaters also bring **silt** from the highlands to the Nile River's water.

During this rainy season, the Atbara contributes about one-fourth of the Nile's water. But during the dry season there is little rain to feed the Atbara. Its current slows, and the great river is reduced to pools of water in the riverbed.

Opposite page: A felucca
on the Atbara River

Plants & Animals

*T*he Nile River flows through many countries. This varied landscape is home to many plants and animals.

A variety of plants grow along the Nile. One of the most common plants is papyrus. Papyrus is a reed. Ancient Egyptians used papyrus to make boats and baskets. They also used it to make the world's first paper.

The Nile and the land beside it are home to many animals. Some live in the water. Others live on the river's banks.

Nile perch swim through the murky water. Nile perch can grow to be six feet (2 m) long. Hippopotamuses and crocodiles also live in the Nile.

The Nile's banks are also home to many birds. Storks, herons, and pelicans nest in the bank's tall weeds and grasses.

Hungry crocodiles in the Nile River

The Nile Long Ago

*P*eople have lived along the Nile for more than five thousand years. Great civilizations, such as the ancient Egyptians, depended on the river.

During the rainy season, the Nile overflows its banks. When the floodwaters retreat, they deposit **silt** along the shores. The silt makes the soil fertile. The Egyptians grew plentiful crops on this rich land.

The ancient Egyptians used the Nile in other ways, too. They traveled on the Nile to conquer neighboring peoples. They moved huge stones on the water from nearby **quarries** to build pyramids and temples.

The Egyptians knew the river's annual flood was the key to their survival. So, they began keeping records of the river's **crests**. They also built canals and dams to control the river's flooding.

*The Rawdah Nilometer has been used to measure
the Nile River's floodwaters since ancient times.*

Exploring the Nile

*A*ncient peoples tried to understand the Nile's flooding. But it was difficult because they did not know the Nile's **geography**. The river's great length and the region's rough **terrain** made exploration difficult.

In later centuries, many people explored the Nile and its **tributaries**. In 1613, Pedro Paez followed the river. He found Lake Tana and the **source** of the Blue Nile. Later, in 1857, John Speke explored the White Nile. He sailed south and reached Lake Victoria.

In 1864, Samuel Baker mapped the river as far as Lake Albert. Later explorers determined the most southern source of the Nile was the Kagera River in Burundi.

Once the course of the Nile and its tributaries was finally known, people again began to look for ways to harness the power of its floodwaters. As the ancient Egyptians did, they built dams.

Samuel Baker

Taming the Nile

*I*n 1843, Egyptians built a series of dams south of Cairo, Egypt. This marked the beginning of modern **irrigation** and flood control in the Nile Valley.

The Egyptians continued their efforts to build dams on the Nile. In 1902, they built the Aswan Dam. It improved navigation on the Nile and provided **hydroelectric** power.

Ugandans built the Owen Falls Dam on the White Nile in 1954. This dam made Lake Victoria into a **reservoir**. It stores water for years when the Nile's water level is low. It also provides hydroelectric power for Uganda and Kenya.

In 1970, the Aswan High Dam was completed in Egypt. The construction of the dam created Lake Nasser. It provides water to Egypt and Sudan when the Nile's water level is low.

Building dams on the Nile has formed reservoirs, controlled flooding, and created irrigation water and hydroelectric power.

But the dams hold back the **silt** that once traveled downstream with the Nile. This reduces the fertility of cropland along the Nile. It also contributes to the **erosion** of the Nile **Delta**.

The Aswan High Dam

The Nile Today

*T*oday, dams along the Nile prevent the annual flooding that sustained life along the river for thousands of years. But the river is still important to those who live in the Nile Valley.

Fishermen catch Nile perch, catfish, eel, lungfish, and tiger fish in the river. Farmers use the Nile's waters to **irrigate** their crops. They grow cotton, rice, corn, and sorghum in the summer. In the winter, farmers grow barley, wheat, and beans.

Communities along the river use electricity generated by the dam's **hydroelectric** power plants. The Aswan High Dam and the Owen Falls Dam supply electricity for farms, homes, and industries.

Though the people who live along the Nile have affected the way the river flows, the river will continue to support those who live on its banks for many years to come.

The Nile River in Cairo, Egypt

Glossary

crest - the highest point that water reaches during a flood.

delta - an area of land at the mouth of a river formed by the deposit of silt, sand, and pebbles.

erosion - gradual wearing, rubbing, or washing away of the earth's rock or surface.

evaporate - to change from a liquid to a vapor.

geography - the study of the earth's surface and climate, its plant, animal, and human life, and humanity's relationship to its environment.

gorge - a deep, narrow passage between steep, rocky walls or mountains.

hydroelectric - electricity that is generated when water flows through huge engines called turbines.

irrigate - to supply land with water by using canals, channels, and pipes.

mouth - the location where a river empties into another body of water.

quarry - a place where stone is cut for use in building and road construction.

reservoir - a natural or man-made place that stores water.

silt - fine sand or clay carried by water that settles on the land after a flood.

source - a spring, lake, or other body of water where a river or stream begins.

terrain - a piece of land's physical features such as rocky, hilly, or steep.

tributary - a river or stream that flows into a larger river, stream, or a lake.

How Do You Say That?

Burundi - boo-ROON-dee
Kagera - KAH-gay-rah
Khartoum - kahr-TOOM
papyrus - puh-PI-ruhs
reservoir - REZ-ehv-wahr
Tisisat - TISS-is-sat

Web Sites

The Nile River
http://www.sis.gov.eg/egyptinf/culture/html/rnile.htm
Read about the Nile River in Egypt's history at this site from the Egyptian government.

Aswan Dam
http://www.umich.edu/~kelseydb/Exhibits/AncientNubia/PhotoIntro.html
Learn about the first dam at Aswan at this site from the University of Michigan. View many great historic photos.

These sites are subject to change. Go to your favorite search engine and type in Nile River for more sites.

Index

A

Albert, Lake 4, 6, 16
Albert Nile 6
animals 4, 12
Aswan Dam 18
Aswan High Dam 18, 20
Atbara River 4, 8, 10
Atbara, Sudan 8, 10

B

Baker, Samuel 16
Blue Nile 4, 6, 8, 16
Burundi 4, 16

C

Cairo, Egypt 18

D

dams 14, 16, 18, 19, 20

E

Egypt 4, 12, 14, 16, 18
Ethiopia 8, 10
explorers 16

F

farming 4, 14, 19, 20
flooding 10, 14, 16, 18, 20

H

hydroelectric power 18, 20

I

industry 20

K

Kagera River 4, 16
Kenya 18
Khartoum, Sudan 6, 8
Kyoga, Lake 4

M

Mediterranean Sea 4

N

Nasser, Lake 4, 18
Nile Delta 19
Nile Valley 18, 20

O

Owen Falls Dam 18, 20

P

Paez, Pedro 16
plants 4, 12
pyramids 14

S

Speke, John 16
Sudan 6, 8, 10, 18
Sudd, the 6

T

Tana, Lake 8, 10, 16
Tisisat Falls 8
transportation 4, 14
tributaries 4, 6, 8, 10, 16

U

Uganda 6, 18

V

Victoria, Lake 4, 6, 16, 18
Victoria Nile 6

W

White Nile 4, 6, 8, 16, 18

J 962   MEI   2/04
  Nile River
  Cari Meister

DATE DUE

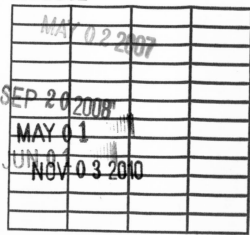

ages 7-12

DEMCO